Letter To The Bold

ese

Cover design by Ese

eBook ISBN: 978-1-7398488-4-2
Paperback ISBN: 978-1-7398488-5-9

A CIP catalogue record for this book is available from the British Library

flow

what could boldness look like in the realms of
love nature intimacy healing playfulness loss
spirituality confidence self insomma life?

in a world where women are taught to hate and fear their
period
where women are bold to reconnect to their blood
my love is for the bold
will you let our love be bold?
hmm?

to think that there are little cute things you do
that someone sweetly admires
without you even knowing

i can taste the intensity of your stare
i'm drinking the burning desire of your unspoken feelings
i see your invisible words clearly
this spell was tailored by the universe
it must be

you thought you had it all figured out
you thought your expansion was all there was
you thought there was no other vibe for your rhythm
you thought your love could not possibly get any more
you thought you knew what the place of oneness was
until i showed up

let me kiss your lips
like god kisses mine when the wind hits

some people are blessed to find true love in their first love
others are blessed to find preparation for true love in their
first love

bold to come
closer
i can’t even curse the time it took us to find each other
the lips you had to kiss
eventually went bitter
preparing you to recognise my taste
a paste that’ll forever
stay
the hands you liked to hold
eventually had to slip away
preparing you for a softer landing
a softer
handling
a thought you once enjoyed having
became just that
once enjoyed having
making room for a mind only the universe could
fathom
bold to come closer
i can’t even curse time
we’ve found each other

- *sweet night*

the way you look at me
the way you breathe me in with those eyes of yours
ife mi
i'd rise for those eyes
the type of love that gazes straight at me
and drowns me in love
over and
over
it looks me in the eyes
and i'm reminded that
all i had to go through was worth it
for this moment of sublime clarity
the determination of our eyes for each other
is a rendition of a higher love

us together
is a love song
us together
is the smile after a steamy reminiscing
us together
is the feeling of a lover's hands in between his lover's thighs
us together
is the desire of more of each other
us together
is my knees getting weak at the thought of what you
whispered
us together
is me rolling my eyes at you
to get you exactly where i want you

i just want to be standing
minding my random business
in my backless long dress
for you to mind the back of my neck
with yo longing kiss
cuteness

isn't it so nice to know that
our bodies are the union of a cosmic coalition

i implore you to surround yourself with people
that encourage self-forgiveness

the universe is at play
i taste like peace
the sun kissed

there are so many things
dangerous about you
and two of them are your eyes

when we cross paths
i do not know the heaviness behind a word you easily spurt out
the heaviness behind a feeling that once weighed your acceptance of it down
the heaviness behind a phrase
you couldn't even
pronounce
yet here you are
welcoming acceptance
embracing the flow
surrendering to the freedom of your
tongue
here you are

the fool feels
the fool does
the fool is
the fool flows

my favourite place
my favourite face
my favourite ace
my favourite taste
my favorite

you seem upset
i am
why is that?
because when you aren't here
you give less
let's say
you aren't a hundred percent
of course
i'm not
when i'm here
i am forced to be perfect
when i'm here
there are eyes above me
when i'm here
i am what you make of me
however
when i'm elsewhere
i am free to be
i'm allowed to make mistakes
free to explore parts of me
when i'm elsewhere
i am ok with ninety-nine percent of me
i am whole and pristine
hundred percent me

- *dream talk*

if you ever feel lonely
look at your beauty marks
they say:
those were the parts the love of your life used to kiss in your past life

doesn't it make sense?
aren't those places you find sensual?
let that be a reminder of how you were loved
and that you will be loved again

if you ever find yourself being oppressed
breathe and ponder the realisation that
the oppressor is actually the oppressed
they must have seen something in you
that made them want to dim you
and just like that
you are
free
take yourself out of the illusion of being oppressed
and allow them to be oppressed

when i'm in your presence
i'm wet mentally
emotionally
spiritually and
physically
but don't get it twisted
i can take my juice elsewhere

i'm excited to see what my version of softness looks like
on you
i can't wait to know you
so i can tailor my moaning to you
i want to unravel my love on
you
i want to see what my version of loving looks like on you
i know what love looks and feels like on me
show me what love looks and feels like on you
then let our love come together and get
intimate
make love to me so i can moan affirmations in your ear
yeah
divine snare
let me moan truths to you
let me moan reminders of how capable you are
i want to hear you moan
let me whisper empowering things to you behind closed doors
in the intimacy of our safety
let me moan affirmations in your ears as we praise god

- love is the bitch

when you kiss me
i want you to taste safety
serendipity
i want you to taste peace
surrender
then when you pull me in
you are reminded of how you didn't lower your standards
now you've found such a pretty home
my lips

a tasteful love
we sit across each other and we savour
there's no waste
our eyes meet and it's graceful
our lips looking forward to indulge
in our sweetness
of our favourite choreography

welcome with softness
versions of you that are knocking to be unravelled
in every phase of your journey

i choose to share myself with you
because i want to
now it's up to you
to want to welcome me
sharing myself with you
and you don't have to

i don't know who can come across such eyes
and not crave to drown in them
have you seen your eyes?
let me speak for them...

your spiritual awakening is your spirit saying
come home
that's enough
it's you choosing your own path
it's choosing to respect your own rhythm
finally allowing god to show what she looks like on you

i'll look at these scars as your kiss goodbye

what color looks good on you
you ask?
me
me colour

letter to the bold

i envy that mic
you pour into her and she alchemises
you give and she receives
you enter and she welcomes
you trust and she never judges
you go to her and she's always waiting
she's your safe space
a place i long to be
i envy the boldness you two get to behold

feel my lips on yours
feel the warmth and the safety that's yours

let me find out how love marks look on your skin
i bet you'll like that
of course

even when you question the universe and ask
are you sure?
not only will it remind you of your worth
but
it will also hold you in its embrace
and say
with pleasure

- *the treasure*

your smile
your dimples
your eyes
your giggles

- *mj*

come
let's peel off layers of our intimacy
let's touch skins of our privacy
explore the treasures of our lack of decency

if the body is a sacred sanctuary
home
then
would you like to come home?

i'm grateful for the strength to release
every ounce in me that fears
surrender
i release

are you upset with me
because we get to spend a lifetime apart?
don't be
in this lifetime
you are this and i am that
maybe in the next
you'll be a particular tree and i the wind
that way i can easily and always find you
even with the slightest breeze
you'll be reminded of my love for you

you are like two unlikely words put together
to make me puzzle and curious
it drives me crazy
and
it drives me crazy

you ask me 'what is your state of mind?'
i say 'you'
you are my state of mind

if you allow me i'd like to wear you...
can i?

no matter how much you love somebody
know that they have every right to love themselves more

i love nature's teaching of acceptance
she allows you to accept her how she is
when you are ready and willing
it is what it is for both parties
intriguing

- *observing winter trees*

the you of today stands on the courage of where you once
stood in confusion
on the shoulder of a version of you in doubts
without a vision
that version of you who stood in the hurricane
and trusted it wouldn't be in vain
even through each pain
she stood for the sisterhood
so when you can
as much as you can
stop and say *you did it*
we made it mama
thank you for the trust
thank you for choosing us

- *wanna know*

everything was put in place to make you whole

give me a reason to write
i am not afraid to write
i wrote you to life

your voice makes me wonder
what version of love this is
it makes me feel
it's safe to be in love
it makes me feel
i am brave to be this loved

- *the bunny harmonising*

it's all been said and done
it's constantly being said and done
all that's missing is your version
so do it your way
with your intuition
get it said and done

behave
you should misbehave inside of me

those silent eye connections
that pull us in
are the loudest
even the universe wobbles
for a min

i am not afraid of the grandiosity of what i'm manifesting
i wouldn't be gifted such freedom of imagination
if i wasn't a body of capabilities and miracle

no matter the lifetime
we find our way back to each other
no matter the appearance
i'd still pick you in each lifetime

i'm enjoying this version of nature
my hands drifting all over your body
like the clouds in the sky
like the wind caressing the green pasture

for as much as i don’t like winter
i respect it
it’s a symbol of the beauty to come

in the process of finding your own rhythm
it’s ok to seek inspiration from other people's

that could give you the courage to recognize and embody
yours

even the waves have their origin
then they break to reconnect to other waves
eventually fading out on the shore
and falling back to that same origin

 - *countless teachings of water*

you are a walking ooze of poetrinspiration
i can write about you all night long
you are the theme that binds words of liberation
my all-time song
you are a constant reminder of why
i love to beautifully put unusual words together
now shift my thong

every opportunity i get
i drown my lips in moisture
your lips are my fav type of balm

how dare i not live my truth?
how dare i allow the world to shame me
for breathing my truth?
how dare i listen to what is external?
how dare i deprive myself of an ultimate vision
that is me and divinely free?

my favourite part of us
was me with a cup of tea
watching you erase yourself out of my life

kiss me
so i can taste what it feels like to be held by the rainbow

i'm not gonna lie
winter sky is pretty
it comes with beautiful trees
it defeats me

every time the universe gifts me a symbol of you
i intend a deep breath for you

i leave crumbs of my essence
on the runway of the universe
for you to recognise
your map to my arms
just tune in first

i enjoy every phase of my life
i immerse myself in the intense phase
and the intensity of the calm days

allow yourself to sink in your light
all will be well and you will be safe
do not be afraid of your own light
and the power of sinking in your darkness

spoil me while you complain about me being spoilt

- *cheeky grin*

no matter how hurt you got
you never lost any piece of you
if you gave them out purely
you are healing your gut

forgive yourself often
anticipate forgiveness
even before the realisation of the need to forgive

wahala dey
for who dey fear to stay alone
wahala dey
for who dey worry for another person matter
wahala dey
for who dey fear to no carry body gum body
wahala dey o

don't underestimate the power of healing yourself
in order to live life and bleed as yourself

i'm building the life i desire
i would have loved to have you in it too
but the universe had other plans

aren't you a beauty in this darkness of yours?
you don't see it yet
but as you grow truthfully
you glow beautifully

letter to the bold

you look at me
like i'm the most delicate of delicates
like you're scared to touch me
because you could break me
but you touch me
because you know that's the safest way
you can protect me

her eyes are so dreamy
like a bed of calm water
if only you knew the profoundness
of what floats underneath
if only you knew

when you lie down with a woman
whose spirit isn't tensed
your experience is intense

when has falling to pieces never benefitted you?
be thankful to who and what shattered you
because they gifted you the opportunity
to piece yourself together
you are your remedy
life's perfect clue

tell me
can you tell when i surrender?

- *sexual intercourse*

i'm not ashamed of my come-up story
without any of those parts
i wouldn't be basking in this glory
mmm

sometimes patience looks like distance and separation

and maybe
you'll be blessed to have people around you
that believe in you
before you believe in yourself
but know that
there'll always be that vacancy patiently waiting
for your belief in self

here
grab my hands
let's go do some breath work

i desire to make you feel things you desire to feel

you walk towards me
and i can taste your hunger for me in your eyes

maybe moments of difficulties
depression and discomfort
reminds us to train our freewill

i don’t want to talk about life in the language that is common
let’s talk about life in the language of miracles
perspectives
your mind's lens
individual tones
energetic flows
silent angles
eye's dangles

i want to be intimately myself
that you begin to question the notion of your reality
i want you to look at me
and you bloom in your nature
i want to use words
that ignite *who are you?*
in you

there's a particular lips
you haven't kissed yet
that will open you to a level of love
that you can't even fathom

you are magnificent
like this extensive sea of clouds

sometimes
i wonder if you are so afraid of the ocean
because you know how dangerous you could be
and you don't want to awaken that beast
maybe you should
yeah
let it breathe

want to know how i feel?
you can find out how it tastes
on the tip of my tongue

i love how god expresses itself through
me
you
and
nature

the pull

to think that the fastest you’ve ever witnessed the cloud drifting
isn’t the fastest
is mind-blowing
do you get it?
there is no limit to you
there is no limit to you

this man cannot have enough of me
he wants to touch me
love me
kiss me
sweet me
profess to me
protect me
provide for me
be inside me
be around
me
he is not afraid of his eruption
for me

can’t wait for you to experience my kind of love
and i pray you are capable of receiving it

i bet you just had a flashback of us
and surrendered to your giggles

amazing
even more amazing
my body
his voice
god
just him

- *prompted*

if you don't trust your body
how are you supposed to trust the universe?
vibration of distrust
is all over your body
and the universe picks on this
trust

i realise how small i am next to the ocean
she's infinite
drifting into one with the sky
then she whispers
baby
i'm just a reminder of how wide
wild
deep
infinite
drifting into oneness with me and the sky
you are

sometimes my conscious mind gets a glimpse of the
divine's infinite love
and experiences a meltdown
and in that moment
all of me is held through it

embrace the tears
it's a reminder of
you got this
or
you did this

have you ever seen love?
no!?

i have
i’m looking right at it

let me remind you of things you once liked
let's recover trails of thoughts you once had

how do you balance your world on my body?
it's the firm grip of your hands on my ass
at the same time
your sweet caress on my chin whilst you kiss me
you reflect balance on me
you remind me of the quarter moon
reliance guaranteed

why do you think people should believe you
when you share certain things
and they think you are crazy
when the first time you had certain realisations
you thought you were crazy!

they say
the sky is blue
because it's the upward version of the ocean

wow
maybe that's why they eventually become one at the horizon
us
you are my sky and i am your ocean

the only purpose you need
is that of being who you are
without fear
show up fully
purposefully

i’m obsessed
with the build up of your smile...

be so comfortable in changing
that you forget how uncomfortable you used to be
work on yourself
so you feel comfortable at not faking orgasms
work on things that deprive you of feeling
and embracing good feelings
you are meant to naturally feel good
don't fight your natural urge
unlearn the unnatural surge

the day the trumpet sounds
is the day you finally see your worth
and realise you have found salvation
by honouring who you truly are

learn to unshame yourself
so you unlearn to shame others
di conseguenza
you'll learn to not be shamed by them

i know what you up to
as i taste your smile
and you test the waters

and as you find home in between my arms
i wonder what it feels like for you
because sinking into you
was long overdue

how can i not love you
when you literally lift me up to touch the stars
and when you look at me
i feel like those same stars?

you must know love
you must know your type of love
you must know how to give yourself your type of love
in order to be courageous enough to give and receive love
i mean you don't have to
but you must

i am the sweetest magic you’ve ever tasted
sono la magia piu dolce che tu abbia mai assaggiato

blue is the colour of authenticity
it's the colour of speaking one's truth
the colour of expressing your truth
being   bold
blue is the colour of showing up
honouring
respecting and acknowledging your truth
blue is the colour of not being afraid to speak for yourself
guilt   free
ridiculously you
i mean
it's true
blue carries the tone of you
blue is the colour of you
and what a view

- *sky gazing*

he said
baby let's make intellectual love
so i read to him
i knew it was you when you effortlessly interpreted me
so i said
tell me
am i your favourite type of poetry?
yeah?
now read me out

will you have the courage to love me
by loving yourself?
hmm?

and when you are full
even the clouds want you to themselves
my eyes want you to themselves
and my emotions have you to themselves

- moonie

experiencing art holds space for courage
it's a reminder of no limitation
of one pulling from source
expressing source
the courage of being you
the courage of just being
it's a reminder to simply   be
the body fulfilling truth
your body fulfilling truth
just be

have you ever looked at someone and asked
how can i love you?
where do i start from?
you exude love all over and i don't know where to taste from

they look right back at you and smile out the phrase
start from my lips

that eye contact is dangerous
i love watching you watch me
you like the looks of freedom on my body
the nooks of your rhythm on my body
i know
i know
me too

sometimes you are presented with things
that you are ready for
even if you haven’t realised
how ready you are

facets of love

it's either:
you know self-love
so you are naturally forced to move away from love
that wouldn't serve you
and that can hurt

or
you lack self-love
and push away love that would serve you
that too will hurt

although you know who you are
a reminder of who you are
can be overwhelming to you too
so imagine what it does to the world

how can the intensity of your eyes
make me grasp for my last breath
and fill me up with life to the brim at the same time?

- *argh the eyes*

have you ever wanted something so bad
it makes you question who you are
it challenges you to unravel
how true you are

i will hold space for your vulnerability
i am a safe space for you to open up to me
with that same breath
are you willing to hold space for how what you say
reflects on me?

as i stare at your immensity
my love is colourful
and you an enticing canvas
where expression is welcomed freely

letter to the bold

i want a love that wants me
a touch that desires me
a heart that is full of me
a body that needs to navigate me
a soul that isn't afraid of me
a journey that is excited for me
a laughter that remembers me
a feeling that can't explain me
a stroke that is uniquely me
a language that is simply me
for me and so much more
because for you
i'll be all and so much more

your eyes
to know that they are capable of undressing me and making me feel powerful in the midst of the world
your lips
to know that only they know
trace and kiss the spots that makes my being shiver
your hands
to know that at every movement they make
every part of my body crave their determination
your wand
to know that a whole package is being delivered with divine service
your voice
hmm let's just leave it here
your body
well
to know that it's home
is soul-warming

when you do eventually heal
and embody your version of love
i pray that whoever gets to taste it
also understands
the journey behind the secretion of pure love

be appreciative to those who played a role
who participated in the process of your unraveling
because without them
without those experiences
you wouldn't have been able to birth yourself
you couldn't possibly
constantly
birth love

look at me with those beautiful eyes of yours
from in-between my thighs

i can only meet you
as far as you allow yourself to receive me

i am grateful for the clouds and how soft
and delicate they are
yet they can portray the dark side of the sky
with ease and when needed

they bring balance
shade

let me bring balance to your world
can i?
could i?
cloud i?

let’s sit in silence and speak the loudest
let’s sink the silence and have the proudest conversation
let’s sink into each other
in silence

my love for you has no borders
i love you in all the languages
in all the dialects
all the signs
i don’t need to cling on to excuses
to not love you
i love you in nature and tradition
simply you

i want to be the reason you are free
the reason why you know love like you never have before
i know   i know
i'm selfish
still   i will be the reason

warmth
let's make love in-between reading each other poetry by the fireside
the flame dare not compare its warmth to that of our bodies
the fruits aren't as juicy as us
we fill the room with layers of our voices
in between breaks
we hear sounds of trust
sensuality
desire
presence
and so much more...
another dimension i dare mention
we can't break this rhythm even with intention

yes
i have a thing for eyes
look at me
intensely
softly
look at me in ways that sing to me
look at me in any moment
anywhere
and the only reason plays in the room
in our world
just us speaking in the language of the soul

- *1:26am*

i like to think that
when the sky decides to shed
i am gifted the first   drop
yes
the universe is that romantic to choose to love me so dearly...

love me
like that first rain drop on your skin

shine on me like the sun does on the sea
there's depth and darkness in her
but he still shines on her
gifts her little waves of sparkles
her own stars
no matter how dirty
he still finds her worthy

when next i am blessed with an opportunity to stargaze
i'll look and keep my focus on you
admire this planet that positioned itself in my life
with the best of intention

- *planet you*

you know
there's an accumulation of your smile in my mind
i enjoy revisiting it often
it's a sacred practice i enjoy
truly

the need to be understood by everyone
is what delays your expansion
peel off the extra layers of people's expectations for your life
and gracefully wear yours
your nature fits good on you

you asked how i was able to do it
i say by listening
i stood still and listened
i listened to the heartbeat of the tree
i stood in front of you and listened to you walk away
i stood in front of you and listened to walk away
my heart pumped and i listened
the words came and i listened
your song plays and i listen
the soul craves
so i listen
your touch stays on my skin and i listen
the veil so thin
i listen for the wind

the time you were gifted to be alone
was needed for you to recognize the sound of your loudest bliss
so you can hear it clearly
when you meet your person

without it
you would trust the butterflies in your stomach

by being yourself
you speak a language that is meant to help someone else
recognise it
encourage them to find their own dialect

i can feel your hand
snake its way up to cup my left breast
to quench a burning thirst

be with someone who inspires you to love different aspects
of your self on a daily basis
who highlights different parts of your body
you never noticed
who kisses different angles on your body
to place beauty marks for you to remember in your next life
who notices new sounds added to your laughter
who saves a strand of your hair
who brushes your lips with a stroke of his thumb
and leaves you blushing
then savours your tongue

that darkness of yours
held a safe space for you to break free
to dance and swirl around
until you felt comfortable to do so in your light

he said *here*
have a glass of wine
she said *there's no need*
i'm not afraid to say things i mean
without a drink in me
rest assured i'll speak up
i'm not ashamed to be bold if need be
you sip up
it's just the universe
you and me

- *intimacy*

i'll give you perspectives that rid of the whimpers
gift you divine knowledge from divine's whispers
spiritually handle your enemies and make them cripplers

- *divine feminine*

what is the best thing to come out of the dark?
you

today i anoint you
i say thank you god for keeping him safe
for his growth and expansion
for his glory and expression
thank you for keeping him safe and not leading him astray
thank you for his mind
body and soul for his spirit
i intend that he may constantly find his way back to alignment
back to himself
i intend that he has the courage to release what no longer serves him
and has the strength to welcome all that is for him
that is him
may he always find god within himself and move as god himself
i intend that he has the clarity for discernment and observes in alignment with his inner being
i intend that he smiles often and nurtures the world with his laughter
may he never shy away from his truth
and constantly welcome his blue sparkles

- *anointing for my lover*

i thought he was my shango
so i danced
i danced to his beats
but i was off-key
he was a disguise of you
a distraction from you
for me to find me
and expand to you
your osun
watch me
as i dance to your beat

you

my shango

- *epiphany*

on mornings when the water is high and close
and the sky is grey
these pink petals look majestic on you
even on days
when your water is low and far from the shore
don't worry
i'll still be looking forward to seeing how the petals look on
you
on your sand
i'll still adorn you

remember how clumsy you used to be with your body
your heart
look at you now
so soft and delicate
oh honey
you're art
what a path

for as much as i know you
i still don't know you
i'm sure my unknown parts of you are lurking at me from the dark
and that's ok
let them watch
observe until they feel safe to share themselves with me
i'll be here to remind them
it's safe to free themselves and be

i took time
so i could recognise what's mine

because you know yourself well enough
because you can be compassionate towards yourself
you are able to hold and extend compassion to the world
as you navigate through
you can extend compassion closely and from a distance
what a breakthrough

me and you
floating in the middle of this turbulent ocean
tell me
can you recognise my tears

if you're aligned with yourself
and that calls for our separation
for you to step away
then so be it
i trust it's good for the two of us

i wish us nothing but pure love
and happiness
one we can't even explain
but orchestrated by the universe

he’s a fucking genius and i am too

i follow the trail of bliss
it doesn’t matter how chaotic
and heavy the path might be sometimes
as long as my eyes are set on bliss
my hands are led by bliss
i am fine and aligned

maybe your innocence is the lamb of god
maybe your entrance to this world was the gift of god
maybe your inner child was the crucifixion that was needed
for you to trace the blood back to you
back to the precious love
maybe your challenges and scoldings were the purity you
needed as proof for the love you carried into the world
for you to remember
for you to know you came from a land of so much more
maybe all of it was what you needed for you to be bold and
change your name from pity
to a lamb of god

- *lamb of god*

in my body of water
all i want to do is scream   and i do
i drown to the loudest silence
the peace
the violence
digging out the clutter

- *cg*

i forgive myself
for moments when i excitingly neglect my needs

love is him putting me in alignment
in my place
so that i can be ordained by the divine's grace
he understood the assignment

do you think lilith was the forbidden fruit adam bit on and then blamed it on eve?

- *fruit for thoughts*

even when you question the universe and
ask
are you sure?
not only will it remind you of your worth
but
it will also hold you in its embrace
and say
with pleasure

- *the treasure*

they say *write about how you find the one...*
i say
what is there to say?
you will see a glimpse of them in situations and people
resemblance and movements
eyes from this and voice from that
as you make your way through life
you piece them together from each face of experience
each gesture breeds theirs
each phase is less mysterious
the closer you get
the truer the clues
until the map is in your face
and your person
in your embrace

or not

the tightness in your hips from the first day
isn't the same as the next

the world's perception of beauty outside of mine is an
imagined place of imperfection
whereas in mine   everything is perfect
exactly how it needs to be

me
my utopia

your body is utopia
a vessel where everything is perfect
everything about you is perfect
you are possible   you command the law of your body
enough

in my utopia
i tell myself positive statements   love affirmations   and
spray beautiful smoke
if i don't
who will?
if you don't
who will?

embody your utopia
breathe and it's created
for if you can imagine it
you can create it
your body will be waiting for you to come home

so allow this memory to begin
amore
don't be defeated
don't be
we'll be living in utopia

- *utopia*

boldness is a leap of faith
boldness is standing up against
boldness is the sweet you taste
boldness is blazing up the place

boldness
is trusting your own pace

boldness is the blue sky
boldness is the sun
boldness is the heart's determination for what it wants
the truest guide

i wish you find the courage to choose to sit with your womb
cry like you've never before
scream like that's all you have left in you
make sounds as if no one exists in this moment but you
feel everything that makes its way from your bottom to your heart
surrender to every sensation that barks in from the dark
surrender to the pain and love of your ancestors
of nature
of god
welcome every wave that streams from every corner of your body
and release at the shore of your face
the flow of every woman before you
and around you
that couldn't but can through you

i wish upon you the freedom that blooms

- the altar

the law of nature is being oneself

nature says
i am bold because i am me
see your reflection in me
the law of nature says *be bold and be free*

- trust me

i allowed source to move through me and did not fear my 'randomness'

know that you are breathing
evolving
growing
expanding
and flowing
know that you are god
and what a be(you)tiful version

~ese~

www.ingramcontent.com/pod-product-compliance
Lightning Source LLC
La Vergne TN
LVHW091318150826
845673LV00006B/1692

* 9 7 8 1 7 3 9 8 4 8 8 5 9 *